Songs Of The Heart

A
selection
of favourite
hymns in
large print

Christian Focus Publications

©1991 Christian Focus Publications Ltd.
ISBN 1 871676 60 6

Published
by
Christian Focus Publications Ltd.
Geanies House, Fearn, IV20 1TW,
Ross-shire, Scotland, Great Britain.

Printed in Great Britain

How good is the God we adore

How good is the God we adore,
Our faithful, unchangeable Friend,
Whose love is as great as His power,
And knows neither measure nor end.

'Tis Jesus, the First and the Last,
Whose Spirit shall guide us safe home;
We'll praise Him for all that is past,
And trust Him for all that's to come.

Joseph Hart

O God of Bethel

O God of Bethel! by whose hand
Thy people still are fed
Who through this weary
pilgrimage
Hast all our fathers led:

Our vows, our prayers, we now
present
Before Thy throne of grace:
God of our fathers : be the God
Of their succeeding race.

Through each perplexing path of
life
Our wandering footsteps guide;

Give us each day our daily bread,
And raiment fit provide.

O spread Thy covering wings
around,
Till all our wanderings cease,
And at our Father's loved abode
Our souls arrive in peace.

Such blessings from Thy
gracious hand
Our humble prayers implore;
And Thou shalt be our chosen
God,
And portion evermore.

Scottish Paraphrases

God moves in a mysterious way

God moves in a mysterious way,
His wonders to perform;
He plants His footsteps in the sea,
And rides upon the storm.

Deep in unfathomable mines
Of never-failing skill
He treasures up his bright
designs,
And works His sovereign will.

Judge not the Lord by feeble
sense,
But trust Him for His grace;
Behind a frowning providence
He hides a smiling face.

Ye fearful saints, fresh courage take;
The clouds ye so much dread
Are big with mercy, and shall break
In blessings on your head.

His purposes will ripen fast,
Unfolding every hour;
The bud may have a bitter taste,
But sweet will be the flower.

Blind unbelief is sure to err,
And scan His work in vain;
God is His own interpreter,
And He will make it plain.

William Cowper

My God, how wonderful Thou art

My God, how wonderful thou art,
Thy majesty how bright!
How beautiful Thy mercy-seat,
In depths of burning light!

How dread are Thine eternal
years,
O everlasting Lord,
By prostrate spirits day and night
Incessantly adored!

O how I fear Thee, living God,
With deepest, tenderest fears,
And worship Thee with trembling
hope
And penitential tears!

Yet I may love Thee too, O Lord,
Almighty as Thou art,
For Thou hast stooped to ask of
me
The love of my poor heart.

No earthly father loves like Thee;
No mother, e'er so mild,
Bears and forbears as Thou hast
done
With me, Thy sinful child.

How beautiful, how beautiful
The sight of Thee must be,
Thine endless wisdom, bound-
less power,
And awful purity!

F.W. Faber

The Lord's my Shepherd

The Lord's my shepherd, I'll not want.
He makes me down to lie
In pastures green: he leadeth me
the quiet waters by.

My soul he doth restore again;
and me to walk doth make
Within the paths of righteousness,
ev'n for his own name's sake.

Yea, though I walk in death's dark
vale,
Yet will I fear none ill:

For thou art with me; and thy rod
and staff me comfort still.

My table thou hast furnished
in presence of my foes;
My head thou dost with oil anoint,
and my cup overflows.

Goodness and mercy all my life
shall surely follow me:
And in God's house for evermore
my dwelling-place shall be.

Scottish Metrical
Psalm 23

Hark!   The Herald Angels sing

Hark! the herald angels sing,
'Glory to the new-born King,
Peace on earth, and mercy mild,
God and sinners reconciled!'
Joyful, all ye nations, rise,
Join the triumph of the skies,
With the angelic host proclaim,
'Christ is born in Bethlehem.'

Hark! the herald angels sing,
'Glory to the new-born King.'

Christ, by highest heaven adored,
Christ, the everlasting Lord,
Late in time behold Him come,
Offspring of a virgin's womb.

Veiled in flesh the Godhead see;
Hail, the Incarnate Deity,
Pleased as Man with man to dwell,
Jesus, our Immanuel!

Hail, the heaven-born Prince of Peace!
Hail, the Sun of Righteousness!
Light and life to all He brings,
Risen with healing in His wings.
Mild He lays His glory by,
Born that man no more may die,
Born to raise the sons of earth,
Born to give them second birth.

Charles   Wesley

Child in the Manger

Child in the manger,
Infant of Mary;
Outcast and stranger,
Lord of all!
Child who inherits
All our transgressions,
All our demerits
On Him fall.

Once the most holy
Child of salvation
Gently and lowly
Lived below;
Now, as our glorious
Mighty Redeemer,

See Him victorious
O'er each foe.

Prophets foretold Him,
Infant of wonder;
Angels behold Him
On His throne;
Worthy our Saviour
Of all their praises;
Happy for ever
Are His own.

Mary MacDonald

Man of Sorrows

Man of Sorrows! wondrous Name
For the Son of God, who came
Ruined sinners to reclaim!
Hallelujah! what a Saviour!

Bearing shame and scoffing rude,
In my place condemned He stood,
Sealed my pardon with His blood:
Hallelujah! what a Saviour!

Guilty, vile, and helpless we;
Spotless Lamb of God was He:
Full atonement - can it be?
Hallelujah! what a Saviour!

Lifted up was He to die,
'It is finished' was His cry;
Now in heaven exalted high:
Hallelujah! what a Saviour!

When He comes, our glorious
King,
All His ransomed home to bring,
Then anew this song we'll sing,
'Hallelujah! what a Saviour!'

Philip Bliss

There is a green hill far away

There is a green hill far away,
Without a city wall,
Where the dear Lord was cruci-
fied,
Who died to save us all.

We may not know, we cannot tell
What pains He had to bear;
But we believe it was for us
He hung and suffered there.

He died that we might be for-
given,
He died to make us good,

That we might go at last to
heaven,
Saved by His precious blood.

There was no other good enough
To pay the price of sin;
He only could unlock the gate
Of heaven, and let us in.

O dearly, dearly has He loved,
And we must love Him too,
And trust in His redeeming blood,
And try His works to do.

C. F. Alexander

When I survey

When I survey the wondrous
Cross
On which the Prince of Glory
died,
My richest gain I count but loss,
And pour contempt on all my
pride.

Forbid it, Lord, that I should
boast,
Save in the death of Christ, my
God;
All the vain things that charm me
most,
I sacrifice them to His blood.

See! from His head, His hands, His feet,
Sorrow and love flow mingled down;
Did e'er such love and sorrow meet,
Or thorns compose so rich a crown?

Were the whole realm of Nature mine,
That were an offering far too small;
Love so amazing, so divine,
Demands my soul, my life, my all.

Isaac Watts

Blest be the tie that binds

Blest be the tie that binds
Our hearts in Jesus' love;
The fellowship of Christian minds
Is like to that above.

Before our Father's throne
We pour our ardent prayers;
Our fears, our hopes, our aims are
one,
Our comforts, and our cares.

When for awhile we part,
This thought will soothe our pain,
That we shall still be joined in
heart
And one day meet again.

This glorious hope revives
Our courage by the way;
While each in expectation lives,
And longs to see the day,

When from all toil and pain
And sin we shall be free,
And perfect love and friendship
reign
Through all eternity.

John Fawcett

Spirit of Grace

Spirit of Grace, Thou Light of Life
Amidst the darkness of the dead!
Bright Star, whereby through
worldly strife,
The patient pilgrim still is led;
Thou Dayspring in the deepest
gloom,
Wildered and dark, to Thee I
come!

Pure Fire of God, burn out my sin,
Cleanse all the earthly dross from
me;
Refine my secret heart within,
The golden streams of love set
free!

Live Thou in me, O Life divine,
Until my deepest love be Thine.

O Breath from far Eternity,
Breathe o'er my soul's unfertile
land;
So shall the pine and myrtle-tree
Spring up amidst the desert sand;
And where Thy living water
flows,
My heart shall blossom as the
rose.

Gerhard Tersteegen

And can it be

And can it be, that I should gain
An interest in the Saviour's
blood?
Died He for me, who caused His
pain-
For me, who Him to death pur-
sued?
Amazing love! how can it be
That Thou, my God, shouldst die
for me?

'Tis mystery all! The Immortal
dies:
Who can explore His strange
design?

In vain the first-born seraph tries
To sound the depths of love di-
vine.
'Tis mercy all! let earth adore,
Let angel minds inquire no more.

He left His Father's throne
above,-
So free, so infinite His grace -
Emptied Himself of all but love,
And bled for Adam's helpless
race:
'Tis mercy all, immense and free;
For, O my God, it found out me!

Charles Wesley

Rock of ages

Rock of Ages, cleft for me,
Let me hide myself in Thee;
Let the water and the blood,
From Thy riven side which flowed,
Be of sin the double cure,
Cleanse me from its guilt and power.

Not the labours of my hands
Can fulfil Thy law's demands;
Could my zeal no respite know,
Could my tears for ever flow,
All for sin could not atone:
Thou must save, and Thou alone.

Nothing in my hand I bring,
Simply to Thy Cross I cling;
Naked, come to Thee for dress;
Helpless, look to Thee for grace;
Foul, I to the fountain fly;
Wash me, Saviour, or I die.

While I draw this fleeting breath,
When mine eyelids close in death,
When I soar through tracts un-
known,
See Thee on Thy judgment
throne,
Rock of Ages, cleft for me,
Let me hide myself in Thee.

Augustus   Toplady

I heard the Voice of Jesus

I heard the voice of Jesus say,
'Come unto Me and rest;
Lay down, thou weary one, lay down
Thy head upon My breast':
I came to Jesus as I was,
Weary, and worn, and sad;
I found in Him a resting-place,
And He has made me glad.

I heard the voice of Jesus say,
'Behold, I freely give
The living water; thirsty one,
Stoop down and drink, and live':
I came to Jesus, and I drank
Of that life-giving stream;

My thirst was quenched, my soul
revived,
And now I live in Him.

I heard the voice of Jesus say,
'I am this dark world's Light;
Look unto Me, thy morn shall
rise,
And all thy day be bright':
I looked to Jesus, and I found
In Him my Star, my Sun;
And in that light of life I'll walk,
Till travelling days are done.

Horatius Bonar

I lay my sins on Jesus

I lay my sins on Jesus,
The spotless Lamb of God:
He bears them all, and frees us
From the accursed load.
I bring my guilt to Jesus,
To wash my crimson stains
White in His blood most
precious,
Till not a spot remains.

I lay my wants on Jesus;
All fulness dwells in Him;
He heals all my diseases,
He doth my soul redeem.
I lay my griefs on Jesus,
My burdens, and my cares;

He from them all releases,
He all my sorrows shares.

I rest my soul on Jesus,
This weary soul of mine;
His right hand me embraces,
I on His breast recline.
I love the Name of Jesus,
Immanuel, Christ, the Lord;
Like fragrance on the breezes,
His Name abroad is poured.

Horatius Bonar

I bring my sins to thee

I bring my sins to Thee,
The sins I cannot count,
That all may cleansed be
In Thy once opened Fount.
I bring them, Saviour, all to Thee,
The burden is too great for me.

To Thee I bring my care,
The care I cannot flee;
Thou wilt not only share,
But bear it all for me.
O loving Saviour, now to Thee
I bring the load that wearies me.

I bring my grief to Thee,
The grief I cannot tell;
No words shall needed be,
Thou knowest all so well.
I bring the sorrow laid on me,
O suffering Saviour, now to Thee.

My life I bring to Thee,
I would not be my own;
O Saviour, let me be
Thine ever, Thine alone.
My heart, my life, my all I bring
To Thee, my Saviour and my
King!

F. R. Havergal

Come, let us to the Lord

Come, let us to the Lord our God
With contrite hearts return;
Our God is gracious, nor will
leave
The desolate to mourn.

His voice commands the
tempest forth,
And stills the stormy wave;
And though His arm be strong to
smite,
'Tis also strong to save.

Long hath the night of sorrow
reigned,
The dawn shall bring us light:

God shall appear, and we shall
rise
With gladness in His sight.

Our hearts, if God we seek to
know,
Shall know Him, and rejoice;
His coming like the morn shall be,
Like morning songs His voice.

So shall His presence bless our
souls,
And shed a joyful light;
That hallowed morn shall chase
away
The sorrows of the night.

John Morison

O for a closer walk with God

O for a closer walk with God,
A calm and heavenly frame,
A light to shine upon the road
That leads me to the Lamb!

Where is the blessedness I knew
When first I saw the Lord?
Where is the soul-refreshing view
Of Jesus and His word?

What peaceful hours I once
enjoyed!
How sweet their memory still!
But they have left an aching void
The world can never fill.

Return, O Holy Dove! return,
Sweet messenger of rest!
I hate the sins that made Thee
mourn,
And drove Thee from my breast.

The dearest idol I have known,
Whate'er that idol be,
Help me to tear it from Thy
throne,
And worship only Thee.

So shall my walk be close with
God,
Calm and serene my frame;
So purer light shall mark the road
That leads me to the Lamb.

William Cowper

How sweet the name

How sweet the Name of Jesus
sounds
In a believer's ear!
It soothes his sorrows, heals his
wounds,
And drives away his fear.

It makes the wounded spirit
whole,
And calms the troubled breast;
'Tis manna to the hungry soul,
And to the weary rest.

Dear Name! the rock on which I
build,
My shield and hiding-place,

My never-failing treasury, filled
With boundless stores of grace.

Jesus, my Shepherd, Husband,
Friend,
My Prophet, Priest, and King,
My Lord, my Life, my Way, my
End,
Accept the praise I bring.

Weak is the effort of my heart,
And cold my warmest thought;
But, when I see Thee as Thou art,
I'll praise Thee as I ought.

John Newton

Jesus, lover of my soul

Jesus, Lover of my soul,
Let me to Thy bosom fly,
While the nearer waters roll,
While the tempest still is high;
Hide me, O my Saviour, hide,
Till the storm of life is past;
Safe into the haven guide;
O receive my soul at last!

Other refuge have I none;
Hangs my helpless soul on
Thee;
Leave, ah! leave me not alone;
Still support and comfort me.
All my trust on Thee is stayed;
All my help from Thee I bring;

Cover my defenceless head
With the shadow of Thy wing.

Thou, O Christ, art all I want;
More than all in Thee I find;
Raise the fallen, cheer the faint,
Heal the sick, and lead the blind.
Just and holy is Thy Name,
I am all unrighteousness;
False and full of sin I am,
Thou art full of truth and grace.

Charles   Wesley

O Love that wilt not let me go

O Love that wilt not let me go,
I rest my weary soul in Thee:
I give Thee back the life I owe,
That in Thine ocean depths its flow
May richer, fuller be.

O Light that followest all my way,
I yield my flickering torch to Thee:
My heart restores its borrowed ray,
That in Thy sunshine's blaze its day
May brighter, fairer be.

O Joy that seekest me through
pain,
I cannot close my heart to Thee:
I trace the rainbow through the
rain,
And feel the promise is not vain,
That morn shall tearless be.

O Cross that liftest up my head,
I dare not ask to fly from Thee:
I lay in dust life's glory déad,
And from the ground there
blossoms red
Life that shall endless be.

George Matheson

Loved with everlasting love

Loved with everlasting love,
Led by grace that love to know;
Spirit, breathing from above,
Thou hast taught me it is so.
O this full and perfect peace!
O this transport all divine!
In a love which cannot cease
I am His, and He is mine.

Heaven above is softer blue,
Earth around is sweeter green;
Something lives in every hue,
Christless eyes have never seen:
Birds with gladder songs o'er-
flow,

Flowers with deeper beauties
shine,
Since I know, as now I know,
I am His, and He is mine.

His for ever, only His:
Who the Lord and me shall part?
Ah, with what a rest of bliss
Christ can fill the loving heart!
Heaven and earth may fade and
flee,
First-born light in gloom decline:
But, while God and I shall be,
I am His, and He is mine.

George W. Robinson

The King of love my Shepherd is

The King of love my Shepherd is,
Whose goodness faileth never;
I nothing lack if I am His
And He is mine forever.

Where streams of living water flow
My ransomed soul He leadeth,
And where the verdant pastures grow
With food celestial feedeth.

Perverse and foolish oft I strayed
But yet in love He sought me,

And on His shoulder gently laid,
And home rejoicing brought me.

In death's dark vale I fear no ill,
With Thee, dear Lord, beside me;
Thy rod and staff my comfort still,
Thy Cross before to guide me.

And so through all the length of days
Thy goodness faileth never;
Good Shepherd, may I sing Thy praise
Within Thy house for ever!

Henry W. Baker

Jesus, my Lord, my God, my All

Jesus, my Lord, my God, my All,
Hear me, blest Saviour, when I call;
Hear me, and from Thy dwelling place
Pour down the riches of Thy grace.

Jesus, too late I Thee have sought;
How can I love Thee as I ought?
And how extol Thy matchless fame,
The glorious beauty of Thy Name?

Jesus, what didst Thou find in me
That Thou hast dealt so lovingly?
How great the joy that Thou hast
brought,
So far exceeding hope or thought!

Jesus, of Thee shall be my song;
To Thee my heart and soul be-
long;
All that I have or am is Thine,
And Thou, blest Saviour, Thou
art mine.

Henry Collins

We love the place, O God

We love the place, O God,
Wherein Thine honour dwells
The joy of Thine abode
All earthly joy excels.

It is the house of prayer,
Wherein Thy servants meet;
And Thou, O Lord, art there,
Thy chosen flock to greet.

We love the word of life,
The word that tells of peace,
Of comfort in the strife,
And joys that never cease.

We love to sing below
For mercies freely given;
But O we long to know
The triumph song of heaven!

Lord Jesus, give us grace,
On earth to love Thee more,
In heaven to see Thy face,
And with Thy saints adore.

William   Bullock
Henry   W.   Baker

Holy Spirit, hear us;

Holy Spirit, hear us;
Help us while we sing;
Breathe into the music
Of the praise we bring.

Holy Spirit, prompt us
When we kneel to pray;
Nearer come, and teach us
What we ought to say.

Holy Spirit, shine Thou
On the book we read;
Gild its holy pages
With the light we need.

Holy Spirit, give us
Each a joyful mind;
Make us more like Jesus,
Gentle, pure, and kind.

Holy Spirit, brighten
Little deeds of toil;
And our playful pastimes
Let no folly spoil.

Holy Spirit, help us
Daily, by Thy might,
What is wrong to conquer,
And to choose the right.

William H. Parker

Lord, it belongs not to my care

Lord, it belongs not to my care
Whether I die or live;
To love and serve Thee is my share,
And this Thy grace must give.

If life be long, I will be glad,
That I may long obey;
If short, yet why should I be sad
To welcome endless day?

Christ leads me through no darker rooms
Than He went through before;

He that into God's Kingdom comes
Must enter by this door.

Come, Lord, when grace hath made me meet
Thy blessed face to see;
For, if Thy work on earth be sweet,
What will Thy glory be?

My knowledge of that life is small,
The eye of faith is dim;
But 'tis enough that Christ knows all,
And I shall be with Him.

Richard Baxter

My times are in Thy hand

My times are in Thy hand:
My God, I wish them there;
My life, my friends, my soul I
leave
Entirely to Thy care.

My times are in Thy hand,
Whatever they may be,
Pleasing or painful, dark or bright,
As best may seem to Thee.

My times are in Thy hand:
Why should I doubt or fear?
My Father's hand will never
cause
His child a needless tear.

My times are in Thy hand,
Jesus, the Crucified;
Those hands my cruel sins had
pierced
Are now my guard and guide.

My times are in Thy hand:
I'll always trust in Thee;
And, after death, at Thy right
hand
I shall for ever be.

William F. Lloyd

I am not skilled to understand

I am not skilled to understand
What God hath willed, what God
hath planned;
I only know at His right hand
Stands One who is my Saviour.

I take God at His word and deed:
'Christ died to save me', this I
read;
And in my heart I find a need
Of Him to be my Saviour.

And was there then no other way
For God to take ?- I cannot say;

I only bless Him, day by day,
Who saved me through my Saviour.

That He should leave His place on
high
And come for sinful man to die,
You count it strange ? - so do not
I,
Since I have known my Saviour.

And O that He fulfilled may see
The travail of His soul in me,
And with His work contented be,
As I with my dear Saviour!

Dora Greenwell

Lord, thee my God

Lord, thee my God, I'll early seek:
my soul doth thirst for thee;
My flesh longs in a dry parch'd
land,
wherein no waters be:

That I thy power may behold,
and brightness of thy face,
As I have seen thee heretofore
within thy holy place.

Since better is thy love than life,
my lips thee praise shall give.
I in thy name will lift my hands,
and bless thee while I live.

Ev'n as with marrow and with fat
my soul shall filled be;
Then shall my mouth with
joyful lips
sing praises unto thee:

When I do thee upon my bed
remember with delight,
And when on thee I meditate
in watches of the night.

In shadow of thy wings I'll joy;
for thou mine help hast been.
My soul thee follows hard; and me
Thy right hand doth sustain.

Scottish Metrical
Psalm 63

My God, is any hour so sweet

My God, is any hour so sweet,
From blush of morn to evening
star,
As that which calls me to Thy
feet,
The hour of prayer?

Then is my strength by Thee
renewed;
Then are my sins by Thee for-
given;
Then dost Thou cheer my soli-
tude
With hope of heaven.

No words can tell what sweet re-
lief
There for my every want I find,
What strength for warfare, balm
for grief,
What peace of mind.

Lord, till I reach yon blissful
shore,
No privilege so dear shall be
As thus my inmost soul to pour
In prayer to Thee.

Charlotte Elliott

What a Friend we have in Jesus

What a Friend we have in Jesus,
All our sins and griefs to bear!
What a privilege to carry
Everything to God in prayer!
O what peace we often forfeit,
O what needless pain we bear,
All because we do not carry
Everything to God in prayer!

Have we trials and temptations?
Is there trouble anywhere?
We should never be discouraged:
Take it to the Lord in prayer.
Can we find a friend so faithful,
Who will all our sorrows share?

Jesus knows our every weakness:
Take it to the Lord in prayer.

Are we weak and heavy-laden,
Cumbered with a load of care?
Jesus only is our refuge:
Take it to the Lord in prayer.
Do thy friends despise, forsake
thee?
Take it to the Lord in prayer;
In His arms He'll take and shield
thee;
Thou wilt find a solace there.

Joseph Scriven

I'm not ashamed

I'm not ashamed to own my Lord,
Or to defend His cause,
Maintain the glory of His Cross,
And honour all His laws.

Jesus, my Lord.   I know His
Name,
His Name is all my boast;
Nor will He put my soul to shame,
Nor let my hope be lost.

I know that safe with Him re-
mains,
Protected by His power,
What I've committed to His trust,
Till the decisive hour.

Then will He own His servant's
name
Before His Father's face,
And in the New Jerusalem
Appoint my soul a place.

Isaac Watts

O, Jesus I have promised

O Jesus, I have promised
To serve Thee to the end;
Be Thou for ever near me,
My Master and my Friend:
I shall not fear the battle
If Thou art by my side,
Nor wander from the pathway
If Thou wilt be my Guide.

O let me feel Thee near me:
The world is ever near;
I see the sights that dazzle,
The tempting sounds I hear;
My foes are ever near me,
Around me and within;
But, Jesus draw Thou nearer,
And shield my soul from sin.

O let me hear Thee speaking
In accents clear and still,
Above the storms of passion,
The murmurs of self-will;
O speak to reassure me,
To hasten or control;
O speak and make me listen,
Thou Guardian of my soul.

O Jesus, Thou hast promised,
To all who follow Thee,
That where Thou art in glory
There shall Thy servant be;
And, Jesus, I have promised
To serve Thee to the end;
O give me grace to follow,
My Master and my Friend.

John E. Bode

I love Thy Kingdom, Lord

I love Thy Kingdom, Lord,
The house of Thine abode,
The Church our blest Redeemer
saved
With His own precious blood.

I love Thy Church, O God:
Her walls before Thee stand,
Dear as the apple of Thine eye,
And graven on Thy hand.

For her my tears shall fall,
For her my prayers ascend,
To her my cares and toils be
given,
Till toils and cares shall end.

Beyond my highest joy
I prize her heavenly ways,
Her sweet communion, solemn
vows,
Her hymns of love and praise.

Jesus, Thou Friend Divine,
Our Saviour and our King,
Thy hand from every snare and
foe
Shall great deliverance bring.

Sure as Thy truth shall last,
To Zion shall be given
The brightest glories earth can
yield,
And brighter bliss of heaven.

Timothy Dwight

The Sands of time

The sands of time are sinking;
The dawn of heaven breaks;
The summer morn I've sighed for,
The fair, sweet morn, awakes.
Dark, dark hath been the midnight,
But dayspring is at hand,
And glory, glory dwelleth
In Immanuel's land.

O Christ! He is the fountain,
The deep, sweet well of love;
The streams on earth I've tasted
More deep I'll drink above:

There to an ocean fulness
His mercy doth expand,
And glory, glory dwelleth
In Immanuel's land.

With mercy and with judgment
My web of time He wove,
And aye the dews of sorrow
Were lustred by His love;
I'll bless the hand that guided,
I'll bless the heart that planned,
When throned where glory
dwelleth
In Immanuel's land.

Anne R. Cousin

Lord, Thy word abideth

Lord, Thy word abideth,
And our footsteps guideth
Who its truth believeth
Light and joy receiveth.

When our foes are near us,
Then Thy word doth cheer us,
Word of consolation,
Message of salvation.

When the storms are o'er us,
and dark clouds before us,
Then its light directeth,
And our way protecteth.

Who can tell the pleasure,
Who recount the treasure,
By Thy word imparted
To the simple-hearted?

Word of mercy, giving
Succour to the living;
Word of life, supplying
Comfort to the dying!

O that we, discerning
Its most holy learning,
Lord, may love and fear Thee
Evermore be near Thee!

Henry W. Baker

No shadows yonder

No shadows yonder!
All light and song;
Each day I wonder,
And say, 'How long
Shall time me sunder
From that dear throng?'

No weeping yonder!
All fled away;
While here I wander,
Each weary day;
And sigh as I ponder
My long, long stay.

No partings yonder!
Time and space never
Again shall sunder;
Hearts cannot sever;
Dearer and fonder
Hands clasp for ever!

None wanting yonder,
Bought by the Lamb!
All gathered under
The ever-green palm;
Loud as night's thunder
Ascends the glad psalm.

Horatius Bonar

There is a happy land

There is a happy land,
Far, far away,
Where saints in glory stand,
Bright, bright as day.
O how they sweetly sing,
'Worthy is our Saviour King!'
Loud let His praises ring,
Praise, praise for aye.

Come to this happy land,
Come, come away;
Why will ye doubting stand?
Why still delay?

O we shall happy be
When, from sin and sorrow free,
Lord, we shall live with Thee,
Blest, blest for aye.

Bright in the happy land
Beams every eye;
Kept by a Father's hand,
Love cannot die:
On then to glory run;
Be a crown and kingdom won;
And, bright above the sun,
Reign, reign for aye.

Andrew   Young

Upward

Upward, where the stars are burn-
ing,
Silent, silent, in their turning
Round the never-changing pole;
Upwards, where the sky is bright-
est,
Upward, where the blue is light-
est,
Lift I now my longing soul.

Far above that arch of gladness,
Far beyond these clouds of sad-
ness,
Are the many mansions fair,
Far from pain and sin and folly,

In that palace of the holy,
I would find my mansion there!

Where the glory brightly
dwelleth,
Where the new song sweetly
swelleth,
And the discord never comes;
Where life's stream is ever laving,
And the palm is ever waving,
That must be the home of homes.

Where the Lamb on high is
seated,
By ten thousand voices greeted,
Lord of lords, and King of kings.

Son of man, they crown, they
crown Him,
Son of God, they own, they own
Him;
With His name the city rings.

Blessing, honour, without meas-
ure,
Heavenly riches, earthly treasure,
Lay we at His blessed feet.
Poor the praise that now we ren-
der,
Loud shall be our voices yonder,
When before His throne we meet.

Horatius Bonar

O for a thousand tongues to sing

O for a thousand tongues to sing
My great Redeemer's praise,
The glories of my God and King,
The triumphs of His grace!

My gracious Master and my God,
Assist me to proclaim,
To spread through all the earth
abroad
The honours of Thy Name.

Jesus! the Name that charms our
fears,
That bids our sorrows cease;
'Tis music in the sinner's ears,
'Tis life, and health, and peace.

He breaks the power of cancelled
sin,
He sets the prisoner free;
His blood can make the foulest
clean,
His blood availed for me.

He speaks, and, listening to His
voice,
New life the dead receive,
The mournful, broken hearts re-
joice,
The humble poor believe.

Hear Him, ye deaf; His praise, ye
dumb,
Your loosened tongues employ;
Ye blind, behold your Saviour
come;
And leap, ye lame, for joy!

Glory to God, and praise, and love
Be ever, ever given
By saints below and saints above,
The Church in earth and heaven.

Charles Wesley

I'm Waiting For Thee

I'm waiting for Thee, Lord,
Thy beauty to see, Lord,
I'm waiting for Thee,
For Thy coming again.
Thou'rt gone over there, Lord,
A place to prepare, Lord,
Thy home I shall share
At Thy coming again.

'Mid danger and fear, Lord,
I'm oft weary here, Lord;
The day must be near
Of Thy coming again.

Tis all sunshine there, Lord,
No sighing or care, Lord.
But glory so fair
At Thy coming again,

Our loved ones before , Lord,
Their troubles are o'er, Lord,
I'll meet them once more
At Thy coming again.
The blood was the sign, Lord,
That marked them as Thine,
Lord,
And brightly they'll shine
At Thy coming again.

H. K. Burlingham

I need Thee every hour

I need Thee every hour,
Most gracious Lord;
No tender voice but Thine
Can peace afford.

I need Thee every hour;
Stay Thou near by;
Temptations lose their power
When Thou art nigh.

I need Thee every hour;
In joy or pain;
Come quickly and abide,
Or life is vain.

I need Thee every hour;
Teach me Thy will;
And Thy rich promises
In me fulfil.

Annie S. Hawkes

It is a thing most wonderful

It is a thing most wonderful,
Almost too wonderful to be,
That God's own Son should come
from heaven,
And die to save a child like me.

And yet I know that it is true:
He chose a poor and humble lot,
And wept, and toiled, and
mourned, and died,
For love of those who loved Him
not.

It is most wonderful to know
His love for me so free and sure;
But 'tis more wonderful to see
My love for Him so faint and poor.

And yet I want to love Thee, Lord;
O light the flame within my heart,
And I will love Thee more and
more,
Until I see Thee as Thou art.

William Walsham How

Amazing Grace

Amazing grace! How sweet the sound,
That saved a wretch like me,
I once was lost, but now I'm found,
Was blind but now I see.

Twas grace that taught my heart to fear,
And grace my fears relieved;
How precious did that grace appear,
The hour I first believed.

Through many dangers, toils and
snares,
I have already come.
Tis grace that's led me safe thus
far,
And grace will lead me home.

When we've been there ten thou-
sand years,
Bright shining as the sun;
We've no less days to sing God's
praise,
Than when we'd first begun.

John Newton

Jesus, stand among us

Jesus, stand among us
In Thy risen power;
Let this time of worship
Be a hallowed hour.

Breathe the Holy Spirit
Into every heart;
Bid the fears and sorrows
From each soul depart.

Thus with quickened footsteps
We pursue our way,
Watching for the dawning
Of eternal day.

William   Pennefather